A Lot O' Granada!
A Kid's Guide To Granada, Spain

Photography By John D. Weigand
Poetry By Penelope Dyan

Bellissima Publishing, LLC
Jamul, California
www.bellissimapublishing.com

copyright © 2012 by Penny D. Weigand

All rights reserved. No part of this book may be
reproduced or transmitted in any form or by any means,
electronic or mechanical, including photocopying,
recording, or by any other means, or by any information or
storage retrieval system, without permission from the publisher.

ISBN 978-1-61477-033-6
First Edition

"*A donde el corazon se inclina, el pie camina.*"

HOME IS WHERE THE HEART IS.

A Lot O' Granada
Bellissima Publishing, LLC

Introduction

The city of Granada is the capital of the province of Granada, in the community of Andalucia, Spain. Granada is located at the foot of the Sierra Nevada mountains, There is a lot to see and do in Grenada, and parents might like to go out at night, and see lots of museums during the day that kids may or may not like; but there is one museum kids will absolutely love! And that is the Natural History Museum because it's interactive! There are also lots of parks where you can go and play and lots of fun souvenir shops where you can see and buy interesting things. You can take a cab or bus to the old part of the city and walk through the gate up to the Alhambra. There is a beautiful and huge cathedral in the center of town, and lots more. This book will show some things you can see when you go to Granada, and if you are looking at this book just to learn a bit about this place, that is good too! With photographs by John D. Weigand and poetry by the award winning author attorney and former teacher, Penelope Dyan, you can't go wrong with this fun book for kids. Look for the video that goes along with this book (on YouTube) to see even more of Granada, and also watch for a Penelope Dyan travel log and kids' show on www.stop4fun.org. As a teacher Dyan likes to paint a picture for kids that will move them toward independent study, and all of these things only make step one on a learning journey that begins with this single step.

A Lot O' Granada
Bellissima Publishing, LLC

A Lot O' Granada!
A Kid's Guide To Granada, Spain

Photography By John D. Weigand
Poetry By Penelope Dyan

You can go to Granada for a
walk in the park.
But kids shouldn't play there
if it's after dark.
Your mother says, "It is always
fun to play,
but today will be a learning day."
Your dad simply nods his head.
You'd rather play in the park instead.
Your dad says,
"Awe, it won't be so bad,
and for coming here you'll be glad!
You will find when all is said and done
that learning is really lots of fun!"

You take a walk from your hotel
and go right down the street.
The pavement dances
beneath your feet.
You, your sister, your mother,
your father. . .
EVERYTHING is close here,
and nothing's a bother!

There is a gate to a Cathedral*
and you can walk RIGHT through
(as long as you and your sister
keep your parents with you.)
Besides, you shouldn't go
ANYWHERE alone,
especially when you're
so far, far from home.

* This is the gate to Granada Cathedral where Queen Isabella and king Ferdinand are buried, and it was built by queen Isabelle after the conquest of Granada on the sight of the Mosque,

The Granada Cathedral is beautiful
and it reaches so high,
that it looks like it's touching
the top of the sky!

You go for a ride and see round
roofs that are red.
There is no place you would
rather be instead.
It reminds you of Aladin,
and of an Arabian night.
As to that your mother tells you,
that you are quite right!*

* The Moslem influence can be seen in the architecture here. which carries with it the influence of the Spanish moors of times past.

At the Natural History Museum*
(in Science Park)
at a grand piano you sit down to play.
You play for a bit,
and then look at Mom, Dad and Sis',
What a glorious, wonderful day!

*The Natural History museum is part of the Science Park, a group of interactive museums where everything is designed for kid participation. Here among all of these museums you can better understand the world in which you live. The different parts of Science Park allows kids to explore from the beginning of the universe and beyond.

You see dinosaur bones
and a whole lot of stuff.
You decide of THIS place,
you CANNOT get enough!

And then suddenly a robot greets you,
as right by him you walk!
You are stunned and alarmed
that it can ACTUALLY talk!
And it appears that
all you really have to do,
is to simply PUSH
on a little button or TWO!

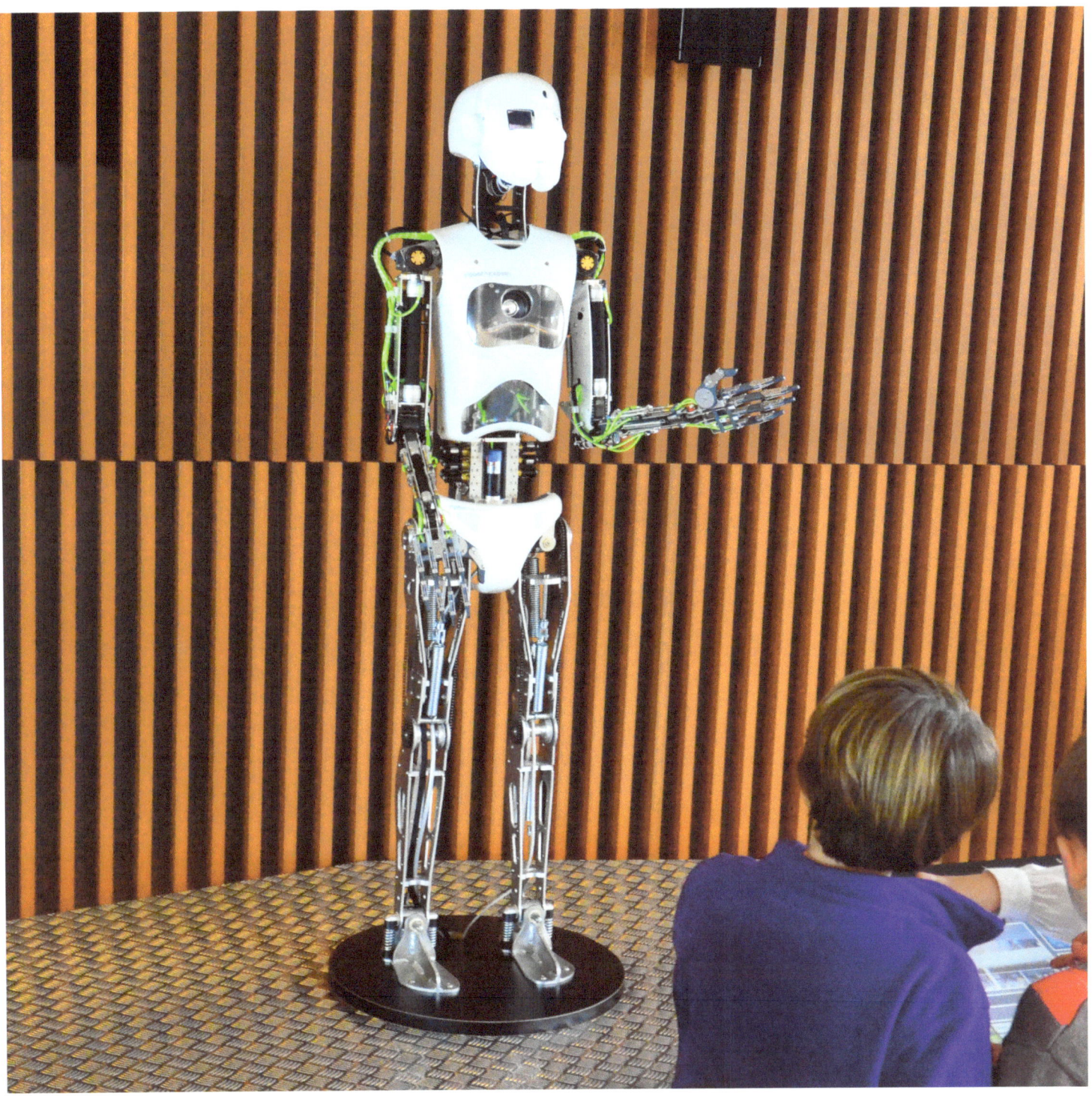

Later, you see a fountain spouting,
and a tall building painted yellow,
and you say to yourself,
"I'm a REALLY lucky fellow!"

When you arrive at an arched gate.
You become excited, and cannot wait!
Mom says, "This is much more
than just a ANOTHER old place."
You look at your sister and shout,
"Come on! Let's race!"
You laugh and you giggle as
through the arched gate you run.
(Sometimes learning history
can REALLY be fun!)
Because history CAN make you wise,
especially when YOU see it
with your very OWN two eyes!*

*This is the way to the old part of town and you can walk to the Alhambra from here, but it is a long walk.

You see something carved in the hills,
small, open, deep enclaves.
Your dad says these are gypsy caves.
Gypsies (once wanderers)
now call THESE caves their home,
from whatever direction
they might decide to roam.
You imagine it is warm inside;
but plainly visible, it's no place to hide.
Gypies dance and sing
flamenco in town,
when from the hillsides,
they wander on down.

You go to another place Dad found,
and you and your sis' look ALL around.
Your mother says, "Listen, my dears,
I don't want ANY running HERE!
We'll go back to the park later today.
Then you'll have your chance to play."
(You and your sis' smile at each other,
just like any good sister and brother.)
You each have a burger and ice-cream
near this place, called the Royal Gate.
And you both finally realize
that for learning and fun and play,
it is never, NEVER too late!

El saber no ocupa lugar.

ONE CAN NEVER KNOW TOO MUCH.

www.ingramcontent.com/pod-product-compliance
Ingram Content Group UK Ltd.
Pitfield, Milton Keynes, MK11 3LW, UK
UKHW060132240426
12048UKWH00002B/6